ALTARS OF THE HEART

DISCOVERING YOUR PATH TO DEEPER WORSHIP

APRIL L. MINGER

Warrior For Christ Publishing
Fort Drum, NY

Copyright© 2014 by Warrior For Christ Publishing. All rights reserved.

Altars of the Heart by April L. Minger

Published by Warrior For Christ Publishing
Fort Drum, NY
www.warriorforchristpublishing.com

No part of the publication may be reproduced, stored in a retrieval system or transmitted in any way by any means, electronic, mechanical, photocopy, recording, or otherwise without prior written permission of the author, except as provided by the United States of America copyright law.

Unless otherwise noted, Scripture quotations are taken from The Holy Bible, New International Version® NIV® Copyright© 1973,1978,1984, 2011 by Biblica, Inc. Used by permission. All rights reserved worldwide.

Scripture quotations marked (AMP) are taken from the Amplified Bible, Copyright©1954, 1958, 1962, 1964, 1965, 1987 by The Lockman Foundation. All rights reserved. Used by permission.

Book edited by Felecia S. Killings of LiyahAmore Publishing
Cover design by Tywebbin Creations LLC
Interior design by Glenda Wallace of Pink Kiss Publishing

Printed in the United States of America

ISBN: 978-0-9903395-0-2

LCCN: 2014908006

This book is dedicated to my husband and children. To my husband, Hura III, thank you for always covering me in the word of the Lord, believing in me, and encouraging me. You are such an amazing husband, best friend, confidant, and counselor to my soul. Thank you for loving me and protecting my heart. I love you!

To my children, Hura IV and Jaylynn, I am so very proud of the young man and young lady the two of you have become. Thank you for your patience and understanding during this process; you have truly been a blessing to me. I encourage you both to always pursue your purpose and keep God first in all that you do. I love you, and I am honored to be your mother.

To my spiritual father and mother, Bishop Cristopher C. Smith and Lady Adrienne Smith, I cannot thank you enough for the teaching and training you have given to me. Your passion for God and His word is evident in the way you live your lives. You are truly an inspiration to me and my family. Thank you for showing me what a truly empowered life looks like.

Acknowledgments

I especially give thanks to my Lord and Savior Jesus Christ for giving me victory in life. I will always give you the honor and glory because it all belongs to you.

Special thanks to my parents who pushed me to strive for greatness. Thank you for loving me and giving me a passion for life. I love you, and I hope I continue to make you proud.

Thank you to my BFF, Constance (Connie), your friendship over the years has been a true blessing. Thank you for all the nine hour phone conversations (ha-ha). Thank you for your listening ears and fervent and effectual prayers. I love you.

To my good friend and mentor, Octavia, you are a true blessing to me. You were there for me during an important transition in my life. Your spiritual guidance started me on my path to a deeper relationship with God and I am so grateful for your God-given gifts and talents. You are forever my Sister.

To my dear friends, William and Christon, you know you are my "favs." Thank you for being true friends (family) always ready to pray with me and for me. Thank you for always having my back, and being honest with me and telling what I need to hear. I Love you guys!

Last but not least, I want to thank all those who have ever offered up a prayer for me and my family. Thank you to all those who have taught me the word of God through: bible study, Sunday school, leadership conferences, or one-to-one talks. I am so grateful for the amazing people that God as allowed to sow into my life; from my heart I thank you!

Contents

FOREWORD	1
INTRODUCTION	3
CHAPTER ONE - The Altar	9
CHAPTER TWO - The Journey	17
CHAPTER THREE - The Heart	25
CHAPTER FOUR - "Arterial Motives"	37
CHAPTER FIVE - The Offering	43
CHAPTER SIX - The Altar Used in Worship	47
CHAPTER SEVEN - Flash Backs	53
CHAPTER EIGHT - The Unholy Altar	59
CHAPTER NINE - The Mind and Heart Connection	63
CHAPTER TEN - Reflection	69
Reflection Questions	71
Journal	79

FOREWORD

"Altars of the Heart" is a must read. In the pages of this book, April Minger takes you on a journey of the heart. A journey that is very challenging, it will cause one to look into their own heart to face the very things that have been holding them back from becoming victorious in Christ Jesus. I truly believe you cannot correct what you are not willing to confront. On this journey, you will discover how to confront the hidden places in the heart where you have not allowed God's power to manifest and bring healing in your life. There are areas in our lives that we have not allowed anyone to enter, not even God. These are the areas of our lives that are filled with pain, shame, and much sorrow. Often we don't realize that trying to close these areas off from God hinders our hearts from being free from fear, and free to worship God in spirit and truth.

April does a wonderful job capturing and illuminating how God doesn't look on the outward appearance of man, He looks into the heart of men to see if faith is alive, and to see His reflection. You will discover, it's with the heart that man believes the Word of God. It is the heart that qualifies you or disqualifies you in the presence of God. It is the condition of the heart that determines if God can show Himself strong in your life. You will be challenged to stop letting the enemy contaminate your heart with the fear of your past failures. Within the pages of this book, she reveals, in the absence of fear, the heart can believe in the miraculous and achieve the impossible. The heart is the center of all creation, but the heart needs to be free from fear to create. When the heart is free of fear, faith comes alive in the heart, and once it is released out of the mouth, it gives things permission to exist in our lives. I highly recommend "Altars of the Heart" to everyone that is ready to confront their past and embrace their future.

Dr. Christopher C. Smith
Senior Pastor, New Birth Church
Pittsburg, CA

INTRODUCTION

What does the Bible say about altars, and what is the meaning behind them? How do the altars in the Bible relate to man today? These questions are the basis behind this book. I believe that the Lord has shown me a deep connection between the altars mentioned in the Bible and the spiritual heart of man. I have sought out the meaning of altars in my prayer and study time, and always felt drawn to learn more about the purpose behind them in the Scripture. I would find myself looking deeper into God's word concerning the building of altars. It was not long before God started to share with me the connection between the altars of the Bible and the heart of man. They share a similar purpose; the difference today is that we no longer have to build earthen altars in which to offer sacrifices to the Lord or to offer worship. We are now able to do this from our heart.

I would take this revelation and begin a journey that would redefine my walk with the Lord; and because of this, I now have a more honest and sincere relationship with the Lord and with other people.

Since starting this journey seven years ago, I have discovered that I had hidden areas of my heart that I would not allow anyone to inhabit, not even the Lord. I would keep places in my heart just for my own personal conversation, and I would journey to them in secret and use these places to help me define, justify, and validate my actions, reactions, decisions, thoughts, and emotions. These places were my own private sanctuaries where I would go to be instructed and guided. These places would represent an altar for me; I had given these places authority and power in my life and I would offer worship and sacrifice to the "lord." These places were not actual locations, but rather past experiences, events that had occurred along the timeline of my life.

Allow me to share with you an example of one such hidden place of my heart. Years ago, a young lady was in the midst of a transformation from a teenager to adulthood. She unwillingly became a victim of date rape. She decided not to tell anyone and tried to forget that this horrible event ever happened. She experienced a wide range of emotions: hurt, fear, shame, and anger. After several months of silent agony and depression, for reasons unknown, she found herself experiencing an eerie "calm," an emotional numbness. This state of mind deceitfully led her to believe she had moved on from the event. She started to date again, and became involved in one relationship after the other, but was never able to find any meaningful connection with the men she dated. She desperately wanted to find a way to connect emotionally, but still she felt numbness inside. She decided to engage in sexual relationships with these partners; however, she realized that the more promiscuous, she was the more unfilled and depressed she became. Then one day, she was confronted with the choices she made when she was re-introduced to a man she had met earlier in her life, but had forgotten. She had once adored this man and wanted to dedicate her life to loving him with her whole heart. She wanted to be reunited with him, but how could he possibly love her? She saw herself as broken and dirty; she had given herself over to a loose and wild lifestyle. She wanted to be loved and wanted to feel clean, but was that even possible for her now? To her amazement, the love of this man would reach passed her sin-conscious mind and deceitful heart, and rescue her from even herself. That very day, she would be reunited with the man she had known and loved from her childhood, The Man, Christ Jesus.

Yes, that day when she rededicated her life to the Lord, she found a sense of peace for the first time since the horrible event. Even though she had been reunited with the Lord, she was still unable to talk about what happened to her. The actual event was only a memory to her, but the effects of the event were still very much in her present day. Intellectually, she knew the event was in the past, but her heart's response kept it in her present; hence, the only way to remember the event was to relive its pain, its destruction, its humiliation, and its power over her. Each visit to this place meant she would surrender her personal worth, self-respect, and dignity. She never thought she would ever recall this event with anything other than hurt and pain. The pathway to this memory was paved with pain and tears, so she prayed to the Lord that one day she would be able to forget it. What she didn't know was that it was not the Lord's plan for her to forget, but to overcome its effects and have victory in its place. She could never imagine a day when she would be able to recall the event without overwhelming pain, hurt, depression, and humiliation; but with a testimony of the Lord's love, healing, and power, she could learn to forgive. The event was not to be forgotten; it happened and was now a part of her timeline. This place was to be a memorial, a place of remembrance, not of pain, destruction, and humiliation, but of God's power and her present-day glory covering in God.

Allow yourself to take a journey with me where we will explore the pathways and visit the places, which we have erected memorials or "altars" within the heart, places where we unknowingly offer personal sacrifices and worship, not to the LORD, but to the flesh. In this book, we will discover the hidden places in the heart where we still need the power of God; every area of the heart where we have not allowed God's power to penetrate and heal. Let's travel through the pages of our own heart and read what has been written by our own hand. What have we said about our life's events? What have we said about who we are, and what God can do? What have we said about why we are who we are and what we have allowed ourselves to become in our today? What is our personal conversation within our own heart? What secret places do we visit within our heart? To God be the glory, come now and reveal the altars of the heart.

CHAPTER ONE

The Altar

We are first introduced to the word "altar" in the Old Testament after the flood. Some may ask, "what about Cain and Able?" Although we see the word "offering" here in Genesis 4:3-5, the word "altar" is not used in any of the 10 most popular translations of the Bible, which include: New International Version, Kings James Version, New American Standard Bible, and The Message Bible. It's possible that some may conclude that an altar was used, but the first mention of the actual word is not used until Genesis 8:20.

> And Noah built an altar to the Lord and took of every clean [four-footed] animal and of every clean fowl or bird and offered burnt offerings on the altar. When the Lord smelled the pleasing odor [a scent of satisfaction to His heart], the Lord said to Himself, I will never again curse the ground because of man, for the imagination (the strong desire) of man's heart is evil and wicked

from his youth; neither will I ever again smite and destroy every living thing, as I have done (AMP).

Do you find it strange that the first occurrence of the word "altar" is found in the same Scripture used to reference the heart of man?

I believe that God is already laying the foundation for the revelation of His word to His children. The earthly sacrificial altar built by a man satisfied God's heart, and because of the sinfulness of man's own heart, God accepted a substitute altar on which man could worship Him and God would release His blessing. Let's go a little deeper right there.

In the beginning, the Bible reveals that God would walk with man in the cool of the day, in the midst of the garden. This interaction between God and man was unhindered; no separation existed between man's worship of God and God's blessing to man. Man not only received the blessing, but he literally dwelled in the very presence of the blessing. Man was covered in the Glory of God; the goodness of God was his perpetual covering day and night. Man was never separated from the blessing in the beginning; in fact, he had no knowledge of anything outside the blessing of God. The fall or separation from the blessing came after sin-consciousness entered into the mind of man, and the heart perceived the presence of sin through the reality of nakedness. The departure of the glory that had covered them revealed a lesser existence outside the blessing. The heart of man was now gripped with an emotional response from the event that occurred. The heart would recall this event with shame and fear, not the same confidence it once had when it communed with God. The heart of man now had a new reference point in which to reflect upon, which would change his relationship with God. The heart that had once only known glory and blessing, now also knew evil and calamity.

This heart was now unable to serve as a place of pure worship; it had been defiled and now a new order of worship had to be established. The offering had to come from without as a symbolic representation of an inner working of the heart in which God would use as a portal or gateway to commune with man. The wickedness of the heart of man continued to distance him from God; and now man's intentions, desires, and imaginations were only to focus on his own life timeline and how to guide his path based on his own recognition of realities and possibilities. Does this sound familiar?

Today, we allow our hearts to be troubled by events, people, situations, and circumstances. We try and figure things out on our own instead of allowing God to direct us. This is the type of behavior that will continue to distant us from God and cause us to miss out on what God has for us. After the heart becomes contaminated by sin, it's no longer suitable to offer up worship and receive the blessings of God.

Noah was a man that, in the midst of a world overcome with depravity and desecration, found favor in the sight of God. It is through Noah that God reestablished His communion with man. The substitute altar was built, and upon it, Noah presented his offering of worship in faith, and God's heart was once again satisfied with the fragrance of worship, and He released a blessing upon him and his sons. It is important to point out what I mean when I use the word "substitute altar." The word "substitute" literally means serving in place of another, functioning as a replacement, provisional representation or proxy. These temporary altars were only a substitute until that day when all men, once again, would be able to worship God from within their own hearts, the day when a perfect and lasting sacrifice would be made by Jesus.

These substitute altars would be used throughout the rest of the Old Testament. We would see the altar used in three main and distinct ways: to worship, to attest to God's power, and to signify the atonement for the sins of man. These same altars would then be a memorial or remembrance of things to come.

> An altar of earth you shall make to Me and sacrifice on it your burnt offerings and your peace offerings, your sheep and your oxen. In every place where I record My name and cause it to be remembered I will come to you and bless you (Exodus 20:24, AMP).

The offerings presented on earthly sacrificial altars were a foreshadowing of God's redemptive plan. God would provide a final sacrifice, one that would be perfect, and abolish the need for a substitute altar.

> For God presented Jesus as the sacrifice for sin. People are made right with God when they believe that Jesus sacrificed his life, shedding his blood. This sacrifice shows that God was being fair when he held back and did not punish those who sinned in times past, for he was looking ahead and including them in what he would do in this present time. God did this to demonstrate his righteousness, for he himself is fair and just, and he declares sinners to be right in his sight when they believe in Jesus (Romans 3:25-26).

Jesus the Christ, the Son of God, is the fulfillment of the foreshadowing. He is both the offering and the High Priest who presents the offering. He brings fallen man back into right relationship with God, not through the legality of the law and continued substitute offerings made upon an earthly altar, but through the heart of man. The Scriptures say it this way.

Here is the main point: We have a High Priest who sat down in the place of honor beside the throne of the majestic God in heaven. There he ministers in the heavenly Tabernacle, the true place of worship that was built by the Lord and not by human hands. And since every high priest is required to offer gifts and sacrifices, our High Priest must make an offering, too. If he were here on earth, he would not even be a priest, since there already are priests who offer the gifts required by the law. They serve in a system of worship that is only a copy, a shadow of the real one in heaven. For when Moses was getting ready to build the Tabernacle, God gave him this warning: 'Be sure that you make everything according to the pattern I have shown you here on the mountain.' But now Jesus, our High Priest, has been given a ministry that is far superior to the old priesthood, for he is the one who mediates for us a far better covenant with God, based on better promises. If the first covenant had been faultless, there would have been no need for a second covenant to replace it. But when God found fault with the people, he said, 'The day is coming, says the LORD, when I will make a new covenant with the people of Israel and Judah. This covenant will not be like the one I made with their ancestors when I took them by the hand and led them out of the land of Egypt. They did not remain faithful to my covenant, so I turned my back on them, says the LORD. But this is the new covenant I will make with the people of Israel on that day, says the LORD: I will put my laws in their minds, and I will write them on their hearts. I will be their God, and they will be my people. And they will not need to teach their neighbors, nor will they need to teach their relatives, saying, 'You should know the LORD.'

> For everyone, from the least to the greatest, will know me already. And I will forgive their wickedness, and I will never again remember their sins. When God speaks of a 'new' covenant, it means he has made the first one obsolete. It is now out of date and will soon disappear (Hebrews 8).

Through Jesus, all men are able to worship God from within our own heart. We no longer need the ritualistic and symbolic representation of the earthly sacrificial altar. The heart of man can serve as a holy place of worship.

I find it interesting that the Scriptures do not describe Jesus as ever building an earthly substitute altar in which to offer sacrifice or to worship. We read about the altars of Abraham, Isaac, Jacob, and Moses; all great and influential men of God, who built altars of great significance. So this led me to believe that if Jesus had built an altar, the Bible would certainly make mention of it. However, the only mention of Jesus making a sacrifice is in reference to him giving his life for the salvation of all humanity. Hebrews 7:27-28 says this in reference to Jesus as the high priest.

> He has no day by day necessity, as [do each of these other] high priests, to offer sacrifice first of all for his own [personal] sins and then for those of the people, because He [met all the requirements] once for all when He brought Himself [as a sacrifice] which He offered up. For the Law sets up men in their

> weakness [frail, sinful, dying human beings] as high priests, but the word of [God's] oath, which [was spoken later] after the institution of the Law, [chooses and appoints as priest One Whose appointment is complete and permanent], a Son Who has been made perfect forever (AMP).

His heart is where He worshiped the Father. His heart was where He sacrificed his own desires to the Father, where He searched for the will of the Father in all he did and said, not only in the public eye, but also in His private moments. In His heart is where He prayed until sweat fell like drops of blood; within His heart He sought strength, guidance, and instruction for the path He walked. In His heart is where He would accept His divine purpose, allowing Himself to become the ultimate sacrifice so that all men could once again dwell in the presence of God with no separation from His goodness.

Jesus always turned to God during His life's journey. He never let anything that was said or done distant His heart from the Father. Jesus gave us the opportunity and the ability, through His life and sacrifice, to follow His example, and taught us that in all things we must trust and rely on God. And just as he learned to do so, we must also turn to God to help us along our journey.

CHAPTER TWO

The Journey

Throughout life, we experience events that we reflect upon and at times may use as reference points or measuring rods. They are moments in time that we are able to think back upon, and come to some conclusion about our life; for instance, the first day of school, the first trip to the dentist, first date, first car, or first job. Each time we reflect on an event, we search our memory pathways with the precise intent to transpose our current moment to a former time; and in doing so, we travel to a past time. The moment in which the mind pinpoints the event and the recall starts to develop, the heart begins to react to the effects of that event. In essence, we reach back and pull the past into our present. The key difference between the actual event and the memory of the event is the presence of hindsight. "Hindsight" is defined as, "perception of the nature of an event after it has happened; the knowledge and understanding that you have about and event only after it has happened" (Merriam-Webster Dictionary).

When we experience life's journey, we are not instructed by the Bible to rely on hindsight for answers to our questions, but we are instructed to seek God for guidance and understanding in all things.

> Trust in the lord with all your heart; do not depend on your own understanding. Seek his will in all that you do, and he will show you which path to take. Don't be impressed with your own wisdom. Instead, fear the LORD and turn away from evil (Proverbs 3:5-7).

We have to stop relying on our own understanding and use discernment or what I simply call, Godly insight. "Insight" is defined as

> the ability to understand people and situations in a very clear way, an understanding of the true nature of something, the power or act of seeing into a situation, the act or result of apprehending the inner nature of things or of seeing intuitively (Merriam Webster dictionary).

Relying on God for understanding of our journey leads us to a God-centered life that draws us closer to Him through our present knowledge of truth. When we respond with what we know and comprehend through

Godly insight, then we will not rely on how we "feel" or by what we see.

All of our life's experiences should draw us closer to God because of His goodness and His love for us. We should draw near to thank Him in times of joy and gladness; we should come to Him in times of need to seek His provision, in times of danger to seek His protection, in times of uncertainty to seek clarity, and in times of sorrow to seek His comfort. There is never a time in our lives that we should distant ourselves from God, but in all instances we should draw near to Him in worship. God wants to commune with and bless His children; however, man allows himself to become distant from God by leaning on his own understanding and leading himself instead of being led by God.

When I began to understand what it meant to draw near to God in all things, and not allow anything to separate me from Him, that was the moment when I realized that God had not forgotten me; He still had a plan and purpose for my life. We understand that purpose is defined as, "the reason why something is done or used; the aim or intention of something" (Merriam-Webster Dictionary). Yes, I had made mistakes, yes I turned away from God, and yes, I even blamed God for my pain and sorrow; but God never stopped loving me. He was still willing to fulfill His plan and purpose for my life. The issue wasn't that I didn't have a purpose; it was that I didn't know how to *walk in my purpose.*

Knowing you have a purpose and actually being able to achieve that purpose are two very different things. Ironically, while I was searching for my purpose, waiting for other people to tell me what I should do, looking for validation of who I am, and allowing my value to be determined by the opinions of others, I discovered through my journey that I had purpose resting on the inside of me the entire time. My purpose was already a part of me when I was created; it was just waiting to be awakened and activated.

What I now understand more clearly is that I was created on purpose, for a purpose, and with a purpose. What that means is this: the reason why I was born far outweighed the circumstances of how I was born. The circumstance of how I was birthed into the world does not matter; what matters is that I was born. I was born to a teenage mother and father, and I was not planned. Some would even label my life as an "accident." But God doesn't make accidents, and it didn't matter how I got here. It matters that I am here, and I have a divine plan and purpose from God.

The secret to living-out our purpose is to draw near to God because it is He who reveals the purpose and gives us everything we need to fulfill it. The Bible tells us in

Ephesians 2:10 that we are God's own handiwork, recreated in Christ Jesus, and that He has already laid out a plan for us and prepared the paths set before us. The same Scripture informs us that God wants us to live a good life that He Himself has already planned out for us. That being said, in order to know and fulfill purpose, we have to draw near to God. But what happens when we distant ourselves from God? The answer to that question is that we jeopardize our divine purpose, that thing that we were birthed to do by God.

Allow me to illustrate further. Imagine with me for just a moment that someone walks up to you, hands you a small golden key, and walks away. Attached to the key is a small handwritten note that reads, "Value this key because it is important and very valuable." You have no idea what you are supposed to do with this key or why it was given to you. What would you do with it? Would you keep it and maybe put it away in a junk drawer? Would you try to sell it? Would you give it away to someone else, perhaps disregarding it altogether and throwing it away? When we do not know the purpose of something, we may ignore its importance. We know that keys are used to open locks; however, that knowledge alone will not give us enough information to see the value of the key. We have to know what lock the key will open.

In like manner, living a life without knowing your purpose is like having a key, but you have no idea where to use it. Knowing our purpose can help keep us on track, regardless of the situations and circumstances we may face. I have discovered that in everything, and in all things in my life, when I have been able to identify purpose, I have been able to find value. For me, it's not about the situations and the circumstances any more, but it's about my response to them and what direction I allow myself to go. Do I move towards God or away from Him? Allowing the events, situations, and circumstances of our lives to distant us from God is how we can get off track in our walk with the Lord. We have to remember what the Scripture tells us in Jeremiah 29:11-13:

> For I know the thoughts and plans that I have for you, says the Lord. Thoughts and plans for welfare and peace and not for evil. To give you hope in your final outcome. Then you will call upon Me, and you will come and pray to Me, and I will hear and heed you. Then you will seek Me, inquire for, and require Me [as a vital necessity] and find Me when you search for Me with all your heart (AMP).

While on life's journey, be careful not to become distracted by situations and circumstances, which may cause you to unknowingly start to live your life through your own wisdom and understanding. Allow God to direct you and lead you through the journey of life; it's not always easy, but it's always necessary if we want to live out our divine purpose and follow the example of Jesus. The Scriptures make this clear to us:

> Imitate God, therefore, in everything you do, because you are his dear children. Live a life filled with love, following the example of Christ. He loved us and offered himself as a sacrifice for us, a pleasing aroma to God…Carefully determine what pleases the Lord. Take no part in the worthless deeds of evil and darkness; instead, expose them. It is shameful even to talk about the things that ungodly people do in secret. But their evil intentions will be exposed when the light shines on them, for the light makes everything visible. This is why it is said,
>
> 'Awake, O sleeper,
> rise up from the dead,
> and Christ will give you light.'
>
> 'So be careful how you live. Don't live like fools, but like those who are wise. Make the most of every opportunity in these evil days. Don't act thoughtlessly, but understand what the Lord wants you to do (Ephesians 5:1-2, 10-14, 15-17).

Our hearts' responses are the key to staying on track and allowing our life's journey to propel us toward God. We can't always control situations and circumstances in our life, but we can control how we respond to them. We have the power to choose to follow what the word of God says, or follow after the sinful nature of our own thoughts and imaginations. We must be careful of the things we allow to penetrate our heart; it's a precious place where we offer worship to the LORD, and in the next chapter we will learn just how vital our hearts are to our spiritual walk.

CHAPTER THREE

The Heart

I have shared with you the importance of the heart's response through our life's journey. We have discussed how we must not allow our circumstances and situations to distant us from God, but draw us even closer to Him. Now that we have a clearer understanding of the journey, let's explore the heart a little more.

The word "heart" is used many times in both the Old and New Testaments. The contextual meaning of the word when used in Scriptures is most often referring to the central or most inward part of mankind. It is used to reveal the seat of one's thoughts, feelings, desires, intentions, imaginations, and even actions. The Scripture informs us that what comes out of the mouth comes from the heart, and the life of an individual is made unclean by what flows from the heart (Matthew 15: 18-19). The heart is the conduit through which our motives and inspirations flow; hence it reveals the true nature and character of a person when exposed and laid open for all to see. The word of God tells us that "as in water the face of man is reflected, so the heart reveals the true man" (Proverbs 27:19). The fact that the heart is not seen from the outside and not visible to the natural eye means that the true intentions of the heart can be hidden from man and therefore can be used deceitfully to garner support for one's own personal desires, whether good or bad. However, throughout the Scriptures, we are taught that the heart cannot be hidden from God; as a matter of fact, we are shown that not only is it not hidden from God, but He actually searches the heart. This fact is vital for our journey in uncovering our heart's "altar." So while the heart can be used to deceive man, it is impossible to deceive God.

When God searches the heart, what is He looking for? The answer to this question is faith. God is searching the heart in order to determine if we are living our life in truth through faith. We are informed through the Scriptures that without faith, we are unable to please God (Hebrews 11:6). Just as in times of old and under the law, God judged the offering on the altar to determine its acceptability; God now searches the heart of man to determine its acceptability. The heart is the residence of faith; it's where faith is found in the life of the believer. It's from the heart that we are able to offer up an acceptable offering through faith. The heart is where we make our lives a living sacrifice unto God and offer pure worship in spirit and in truth through faith.

The Scriptures provide us a very clear distinction between the acceptable practices under the law and the role of faith.

> Oh, foolish Galatians! Who has cast an evil spell on you? For the meaning of Jesus Christ's death was made as clear to you as if you had seen a picture of his death on the cross. Let me ask you this one question: Did you receive the Holy Spirit by obeying the Law of Moses? Of course not! You received the Spirit because you believed the message you heard about Christ. How foolish can you be? After starting your Christian lives in the Spirit, why are you now trying to become perfect by your own human effort? Have you experienced so much for nothing? Surely it was not in vain, was it? I ask you again, does God give you the Holy Spirit and work miracles among you because you obey the law? Of course not! It is because you believe the message you heard about Christ. In the same way, 'Abraham believed God, and God counted him as righteous because of his faith.' The real children of Abraham, then, are those who put their faith in God. What's more, the Scriptures looked forward to this time when God would declare the Gentiles to be righteous because of their faith. God proclaimed this good news to Abraham long ago when he said, 'All nations will be blessed through you.' So all who put their faith in Christ share the same blessing Abraham received because of his faith. But those who depend on the law to make them right with God are under his curse, for the Scriptures say, 'Cursed is everyone who does not observe and obey all the

commands that are written in God's Book of the Law.' So it is clear that no one can be made right with God by trying to keep the law. For the Scriptures say, 'It is through faith that a righteous person has life.' This way of faith is very different from the way of law, which says, 'It is through obeying the law that a person has life' but Christ has rescued us from the curse pronounced by the law. When he was hung on the cross, he took upon himself the curse for our wrongdoing. For it is written in the Scriptures, 'Cursed is everyone who is hung on a tree.' Through Christ Jesus, God has blessed the Gentiles with the same blessing he promised to Abraham, so that we who are believers might receive the promised Holy Spirit through faith (Galatians 3:1-14).

The heart qualifies or disqualifies us for the presence and power of God in our life. But let's explore that statement and get more understanding on why this is true in line with the Scriptures.

Again, we have to look back to the beginning, to the book of Genesis. God saw the thoughts, intentions, and imaginations of man's heart, which was continually evil; therefore man was disqualified from the physical presence of God, but Noah was not disqualified because his heart was faithful toward Him, and he found favor.

> [Prompted] by faith Noah, being forewarned by God concerning events of which as yet there was no visible sign, took heed *and* diligently *and* reverently constructed *and* prepared an ark for the deliverance of his own family. By this [his faith which relied on

God] he passed judgment *and* sentence on the world's unbelief and became an heir *and* possessor of righteousness that relation of being right into which God puts the person who has faith (Hebrews 11:7, AMP).

We can also see the same principle used in Deuteronomy the eighth chapter: God searches, tests, and proves the heart to reveal the true intentions of man to obey his commands. He also shows man that he must keep careful watch over his own heart because it can be deceived and cause man to believe that he can live by the works of his own hands and through the power of his own will, thus disqualifying him from the presence and power of God from working in his life. We also see in the book of 1 Samuel 16:7 a very clear picture of the role of the heart in qualifying David to be chosen as king. Here, God tells Samuel to not rely on his own ability to look upon the appearance of man, the outward qualifications, but rather rely on Him for the choosing of who was to be blessed and anointed the next King of Israel. God told Samuel that he must rely on Him because He looks not on the outward appearance, but rather at the heart. In another example, it was because Solomon turned his heart away from God that he disqualified himself in the eyes of the Lord, and the Kingdom was rent from his hands and given to another (1 Kings 11:4-11).

To further our understanding of the significance of the heart, let's take a look at it from the natural realm. The physical heart is a pump made of muscle that transports blood throughout the body so it can provide every living cell vital life-sustaining nutrients while cleaning up the waste. The heart is the conduit of the entire body; all the blood in the human body must flow to it, through it, and from it in order for a person to live; the entire body is dependent on the function of the heart.

The heart cannot be seen from outside the body, but it can be evidenced by the nature of its function. The functioning heart causes detectable signs within the body; these signs include a pulse and a blood pressure, both of which can be measured and used to gauge the healthiness or condition of the heart and the body. The condition of the heart is important because it is how the blood is able to reach every living cell in the body, from the skin to the brain; therefore, anything that hinders the function of the heart threatens the entire body. The importance of the heart becomes even clearer when we are informed by the American Heart Association that heart disease is the leading cause of death for both men and women in the United States. Conditions of the heart left untreated can, and often do, result in death.

The heart, when not functioning properly, can also be evidenced by the symptoms it produces. The body will not function well; it's sluggish and easily tired due to decreased oxygen and other nutrients, and it feels weak and dizzy. The body can experience pain and discomfort when doing the smallest of task and daily activities. To detect conditions of the physical heart, there are tests that the medical professional will have you undergo. These tests reveal what's really going on with the heart, and even the subtle inconsistencies can be revealed with more complex tests.

Much like the physical heart, the spiritual heart has the important task of carrying the blood to every part of the body. The blood is that of Christ, and the body is the true church. The Bible tells us that we are saved through our confession of faith in the power of the blood of Christ. The blood of Christ (the Lamb of God) brings life to man, cleansing him of sin and making him alive through the nutrients it supplies to the spiritual body. This heart must function properly so as to provide the life-sustaining flow of grace and mercy in the life of man. Through the blood of Christ, we are made alive spiritually, and like the physical heart that must function to sustain physical life, the spiritual heart must function to sustain spiritual life.

The spiritual heart is also evidenced by how well it functions. The functioning spiritual heart also causes detectable signs within the body or church. Love and faith can be measured and used to gauge the health and condition of the spiritual heart. Love is the first sign of those who are spiritually alive; and just as a first responder will check for a pulse to signify life-sustaining function of the physical heart, God also checks the spiritual heart for function based on our love for Him and for one another.

> Dear friends, let us continue to love one another, for love comes from God. Anyone who loves is a child of God and knows God. But anyone who does not love does not know God, for God is love. God showed how much he loved us by sending his one and only Son into the world so that we might have eternal life through him. This is real loved — not that we loved God, but that he loved us and sent his Son as a sacrifice to take away our sins. Dear friends, since God loved us that much, we surely ought to love each other. No one has ever seen God. But if we love each other, God lives in us, and his love is brought to full expression in us. And God has given us his Spirit as proof that we live in him and he in us. Furthermore, we have seen with our own eyes and now testify that the Father sent his Son to be the Savior of the world. All who confess that Jesus is the Son of God have God living in them, and they live in God. We know how much God loves us, and we have put our trust in his love. God is love, and all who live in love live in God, and God lives in them. And as we live in God, our love grows more perfect. So we will not be afraid on the Day of Judgment, but we can face him with confidence because we live like Jesus here in this world. Such love has no fear, because perfect love expels all fear. If we are afraid, it is for fear of punishment, and this shows that we have not fully

experienced his perfect love. We love each other because he loved us first. If someone says, 'I love God,' but hates a Christian brother or sister, that person is a liar; for if we don't love people we can see, how can we love God, whom we cannot see? And he has given us this command: Those who love God must also love their Christian brothers and sisters (1 John 4:7-21).

Faith is to the spiritual heart what blood pressure is to the physical heart; it gives a measurement of the power or force of the blood flowing through the body; but unlike the physical heart, which cannot handle a high pressure flow without causing damage, the spiritual heart has an unlimited capacity to believe in the power of the word of God.

Our faith is evidenced by our actions; the Bible informs us that faith without works is dead or unfruitful in our lives. The more we use our faith, the stronger and more powerful it becomes. The stronger our faith becomes, the greater the functionality of the spiritual heart.

The spiritual heart that suffers from a lack of love and faith will also show detectable symptoms in the life of the individual. Spiritually, they will be weak and lack the ability to witness to the lost. They will once again be ruled by impulsive behaviors, relying on their own sensual lust. They will become distracted by their own pain and discomfort and unable to be used by God to heal the pain of others; and they will be over-sensitive and prone to offenses and strife with others. The spiritual heart has to be able to function unhindered in order to supply the individual with what they need, and when it cannot, the "body," or church as a whole, will suffer.

> Therefore I, a prisoner for serving the Lord, beg you to lead a life worthy of your calling, for you have been called by God. Always be humble and gentle. Be patient with each other, making allowance for each other's faults because of your love. Make every effort to keep yourselves united in the Spirit, binding yourselves together with peace. For there is one body and one Spirit, just as you have been called to one glorious hope for the future. There is one Lord, one faith, one baptism, and one God and Father, who is over all and in all and living through all.
>
> Now these are the gifts Christ gave to the church: the apostles, the prophets, the evangelists, and the pastors and teachers. Their responsibility is to equip God's people to do his work and build up the church, the body of Christ. This will continue until we all come to such unity in our faith and knowledge of God's Son that we will be mature in the Lord, measuring up to the full and complete standard of Christ. Then we will no longer be immature like children. We won't be tossed and blown about by every wind of new teaching. We will not be influenced when people try to trick us with lies so clever they sound like the truth. Instead, we will speak the truth in love, growing in every way more and more like Christ, who is the head of his body, the church. He makes the whole body fit together perfectly. As each part does its own special work, it helps the other parts grow, so

that the whole body is healthy and growing and full of love. So stop telling lies. Let us tell our neighbors the truth, for we are all parts of the same body. And 'don't sin by letting anger control you.' Don't let the sun go down while you are still angry, for anger gives a foothold to the devil. If you are a thief, quit stealing. Instead, use your hands for good hard work, and then give generously to others in need. Don't use foul or abusive language. Let everything you say be good and helpful, so that your words will be an encouragement to those who hear them. And do not bring sorrow to God's Holy Spirit by the way you live. Remember, he has identified you as his own, guaranteeing that you will be saved on the day of redemption. Get rid of all bitterness, rage, anger, harsh words, and slander, as well as all types of evil behavior. Instead, be kind to each other, tenderhearted, forgiving one another, just as God through Christ has forgiven you (Ephesians 4:1-4, 11-16, 25-32).

We must take personal inventory of our spiritual heart, because God will test it in order to reveal its true condition. Is it able to function without hindrances? Are we easily offended by others? Are we able to witness to the lost without becoming distracted by our own situations? Do we operate in love and faith? Do we do things from a place of sincere and honest motives, or do we do them with hopes that we will further or own agendas? In the following chapter, we will examine how our heart's motives dictate our actions and behaviors.

CHAPTER FOUR

"Arterial Motives"

What are arterial motives? It is what I use to describe the selfish and self-centered choices one makes in order to further their own agenda; these are the building blocks for an "unholy" altar. (The phrase "ulterior motives" would mean the same thing as my use of "arterial motives." I am making reference to the heart.) Through these "arterial motives" come such things as manipulation, deceit, lies, twisting, misrepresentation, self-pity, self-hate, false humility, fear, exaggerations, indulgent behaviors, and personal exhortations, all used to garner support for our ambitions and self-proclaimed purpose. We will often become easily offended and cutoff anyone who dares to question our behavior; we will defend our attitude no matter what anyone has to say. We will walk away from friends and family just for the sake of "proving we are right." The truth is we are actually using "arterial motives" to excuse our offended heart, which allows us to harbor things like un-forgiveness, anger, and fear. These hidden motives deceitfully cause us to "feel" validated in our faithless and loveless response to people and life's events. This is where our hearts become hardened and unable to offer true worship, and our communion with God is hindered. This is the plan of the enemy; he wants us to keep our hearts in this condition so we won't be able to experience the blessing that comes from worshiping God in Spirit and truth.

> If you are wise and understand God's ways, prove it by living an honorable life, doing good works with the humility that comes from wisdom. But if you are bitterly jealous and there is selfish ambition in your heart, don't cover up the truth with boasting and lying. For jealousy and selfishness are not God's kind of wisdom. Such things are earthly, unspiritual, and demonic. For wherever there is jealousy and selfish ambition, there you will find disorder and evil of every kind. But the wisdom from above is first of all pure. It is also peace loving, gentle at all times, and willing to yield to others. It is full of mercy and good deeds. It shows no favoritism and is always sincere. And those who are peacemakers will plant seeds of peace and reap a harvest of righteousness (James 3:13-18).

If we allow these self-serving motives to lead and direct us, we will stop the word of God from flowing in our lives. We won't fully operate in our purpose and understand the process of our life's journey.

Once the heart is ruled by self-inspired desires, it is no longer available to receive insight of God's truth, and the individual runs the risk of missing the opportunity God has waiting for them. The Bible says it this way:

> Better is a poor man who walks in his integrity than a rich man who is perverse in his speech and is a self-confident fool. Desire without knowledge is not good, and to be overhasty is to sin and miss the mark. The foolishness of man subverts his way ruins his affairs; then his heart is resentful and frets against the Lord (Proverbs 19: 1-3).

This is why the enemy wants to deceive man into relying on his own works, thoughts, motives, and desires. When we fail to rely on God in faith, we become overwhelmed with the cares of this world; our hearts then become resentful towards God. We blame God for our own shortcomings and turn away from Him.

"The heart is above all deceitful…" These words are a very stern warning about the sinful, self-serving capabilities of the heart. The unrestored heart is fertile ground for un-forgiveness, anger, fear, doubt, distrust, and unbelief. When our hearts are polluted with the cares and worries of life, it becomes depressed and burdened. And we are not able to operate in faith when our hearts are in this condition. The deceived heart frets against the Lord; it mourns the past, miscarries the present, and doubts the future. It causes the individual to experience regret regarding people and events of the past; it fails to see the significance of their present opportunities, and offers no hope for things to come in their future, all because it's overcome with the cares of the world; there is no room for faith to operate in their lives.

Regret stems from deep sorrow or emotional pain that we have held onto from our past. When people cause us pain, we often replay it over and over in our mind until it eventually works its way into our heart. Once in the heart, it turns into un-forgiveness. For example, when someone does or says something to us that causes pain, we feel the initial effects. We reason in our mind, and make a determination as to how we will respond in that moment. If in the moments that follow we are able to recover from it through forgiveness, then the heart is protected from its effects. On the other hand, if we don't operate in the power of forgiveness and allow the situation to play over and over in our mind, the heart will respond with un-forgiveness. Once un-forgiveness is in our hearts, it leads us away from God because we close ourselves off from His grace.

> Since God chose you to be the holy people he loves, you must clothe yourselves with tenderhearted mercy, kindness, humility, gentleness, and patience. Make allowance for each other's faults, and forgive anyone who offends you. Remember, the Lord forgave you, so you must forgive others. Above all, clothe yourselves with love, which binds us all together in perfect harmony. And let the peace that comes from Christ rule in your hearts. For as members of one body you are called to live in peace. And always be thankful. Let the message about Christ, in all its richness, fill your lives. Teach and counsel each other with all the wisdom he gives. Sing psalms and hymns and spiritual songs to God with thankful hearts. And whatever you do or say, do it as a representative of the Lord Jesus, giving thanks through him to God the Father (Colossians 3:12-17).

The only regret we experience should be godly sorrow for our sins, which lead us to repentance. We should not allow regret to have an exalted place in our hearts which leads us to experience despair. The moment we start to experience the emotional symptoms of despair, our hearts become polluted. The polluted heart has no hope for the things to come, neither the ability to celebrate the things that are here. This heart is diseased and cannot function properly. This heart is a laboratory for producing toxic relationships and unhealthy bonds to both people and things. Do you remember my story that I shared with you at the beginning of this book? How after being an unwilling victim of date rape, I wanted to connect emotionally with a partner, but could not. I also shared with you how I tried creating the connection by engaging in sexual activities; well, this was because I had developed unhealthy bonds due to giving years of my life to un-forgiveness, fear, shame, and anger.

After taking this journey with me, you may find that you also have areas in your heart that produce unhealthy bonds. This heart is sick with insecurities, disappointments, and distrust. The power of love and faith in God can break every un-healthy bond, and free you from all unholy altars in your heart. The question that you have to answer is, will you submit to the process? You can be free from the bondage of your past if you are willing to give it to God.

CHAPTER FIVE

The Offering

What are we offering to the Lord? Earlier I mentioned that I had discovered that I had hidden areas of my heart. These were secret places just for me; I would seek validation for my life choices in these places. I was not relying on God for guidance, but rather, my own past experiences. I directed my own path based on how I felt; my expectations were based on past pain and fear. I had given these places authority and power in my life. I allowed these places to become an altar of sacrifice; I would relinquish my freedom in God, my identity, and my purpose. This was not an easy thing to uncover because it required me to face the truth. What truth? The truth that I am a not a default product of my environment! What does that mean? I had to admit that I was created on purpose, for a purpose, by God, not by circumstances, and I have responsibilities for who I become. Yes, I have been exposed to influences, but I'm the one accountable for the path I choose to take, regardless of the five W's (who, what, when, where, and why) in my life. I have the power of choice, and what I do with it is up to me. This is not going to be popular for some people to read because it does not allow for excuses that may forge from self-pity or self-deprecation. It does not allow us to continue in our poor behavior or to make bad choices because of our past experiences. It does not allow for us to harbor hatred, malice, anger, or un-forgiveness in our heart.

This is a hard truth, but the truth nonetheless. I had to confess that I had used events in my past to excuse my present failings and shortcomings. This is why the heart can be so deceitful; it is capable of such manipulations, both against others and itself. When we do not allow ourselves to face the truth, we choose to remain captive to the past, and we are unable to experience the true life available to us in God. To face the truth means that I now am responsible for the life I live and the outcome of the choices I now make. When we stop looking for ways to excuse our lack of commitment to God, we will find our purpose in God! This is the moment in which we can bring a holy and acceptable offering unto the Lord; the offering of true worship, not the emotional pangs of a wounded heart that suffers from the lack of true commitment to the Lord. When we are able to face this truth and really commit to the Lord, we no longer feel the need to hide from His presence; rather, we desire it even more, and we begin to search our own heart for anything that would threaten or hinder our ability to draw closer to Him. King David said it this way in the Scriptures:

> Behold, You desire truth in my inmost heart. Purify me with hyssop, and I shall be clean; wash me, and I shall be whiter than snow. Make me to hear joy and gladness and be satisfied; let the bones which you have broken rejoice. Hide your face from my sins and blot out all my guilt and iniquities. Create in me a clean heart, O God, and renew a right spirit within me. Cast me not away from your presence and take not Your Holy Spirit from me. My sacrifice to God is a broken spirit; a broken and a contrite heart, such O God, You will not despise (Psalm 51: 6-11; 17).

This is the moment in which we exchange the unholy for the holy offering; we realize that we only have an inferior offering; but in Christ we have the superior, everlasting offering, acceptable and holy unto God. This exchange creates the fragrance of true worship as it arises from the altar of the heart. Let's explore this concept further as we move into the next chapter, and study how the altars were used in worship.

CHAPTER SIX

The Altar Used in Worship

To understand the significance of the use of the altar in worship, we should take a closer look at the word "worship," and take an opportunity to dig deeper into its meaning in the Scripture. Worship as used in the Old Testament means to "bow down" or "to prostrate oneself." This word appears in Genesis in reference to Abraham going up Mount Moriah to sacrifice a burnt offering to God.

> And Abraham said to his servants settle down and stay here with the donkey, and I and the young man will go yonder and worship and come again to you (Genesis 22:5, AMP).

Looking at only one section of the Scripture fails to show the complete significance of this passage; hence, it is vital to read verse five in context with the rest of the passage. In Genesis 22:1-18, this passage tells us that God tested and proved Abraham through worship. God asked Abraham to take his only son (beloved and true heir), Isaac, and offer him up as a burnt offering. Abraham prepared for the journey, gathering all necessary supplies as God had asked and left for the region of Moriah, which was about a three-day trip. The fact that Abraham had to embark on a journey is of extreme importance, for the journey was as important as the event.

Abraham was on a journey, which appeared to be filled with grim consequences: he was going to kill his son. The journey would seem to be one of grave circumstances and one in which Abraham would feel great sorrow, but Abraham had something that he could hold onto. God had promised Abraham that through Isaac, He was going to bless him and establish His everlasting covenant with him and his seed after him. This hope had to be on Abraham's mind as they made the three-day journey. The trip was a heart conversation between Abraham and God. Abraham must have recounted the words God had spoken to him concerning the future and how he would bless him, but now he had to step in faith and believe God for what he must do in this present moment.

Abraham sought God and found peace in his own heart about what would take place on the mountain, and surely God had already provided the means for all that

He had said concerning the life of Abraham and his son, Isaac. Once they reached the end of the three-day trip, Abraham's heart was in such peace and was rejoicing in God that he was able to call the offering worship. He pronounced to his servants what his heart had been contemplating throughout the journey: that on this mountain, he would worship and God would show up in a mighty way; that in this moment, God would provide. The altar that was built in this place was a reminder, a memorial of God's provision for the completeness and fulfillment of His promise, both now and forever. When man's heart finds peace in God's word, he will look up and see a place to worship, even if the journey that led him there seemed grim and empty of God's grace at the start.

The heart has the ability to seek God in the darkest moment and in the face of intense pressure. There will be times that make us feel as though we should give up, but when we worship God from the altar, we allow our life to transcend the natural realm and link up with the heavenly or supernatural realm. We can use our Godly insight, and see what God has already done (the end result), and as a result we can rejoice and rest in the journey. This is what Abraham tapped into while he embarked on his three-day journey.

The Bible tells us in the book of Hebrews 10:22-23:

> Let us all come forward and draw near with true (honest and sincere) hearts in unqualified assurance and absolute conviction engendered by faith (by that leaning of the entire human personality on God in absolute trust and confidence in His power, wisdom, and goodness), having our hearts sprinkled and purified from a guilty (evil) conscience and our bodies cleansed with pure water. So let us seize and hold fast and retain without wavering the hope we cherish and confess and our acknowledgement of it, for He Who promised is reliable (sure) and faithful to His word (AMP).

Although this passage had not been written until many generations after Abraham had already lived and died, Abraham had something that allowed him to operate in it. Abraham had established his heart in faith and his conviction produced faith; hence, he was known in Scripture and in the modern day church as the father of faith. Faith is an essential element of worship because it brings us into agreement with who God is and what He is doing. This is an important place for us to pause and take a minute to understand why this is vital in dealing with the heart.

The Bible tells us that the heart is the center of our mental, emotional, and moral character. If the heart is plagued with unbelief, the whole body will suffer.

> I will bless the Lord, Who has given me counsel; yes, my heart instructs me in the night seasons. I have set the Lord continually

before me; because He is at my right hand, I shall not be moved. Therefore my heart is glad and my glory [my inner self] rejoices; my body too shall rest *and* confidently dwell in safety (Psalm 16:7-9, AMP).

The word of God also tells us that without faith, it's impossible to please God; therefore, in order to worship with sincerity and honesty, we must worship in faith.

If the heart is polluted then we are hindered with regard to how we are able to receive from God. We are like a cup with holes that cannot be filled; we see everyone around us being blessed and overcoming trouble and yet we are still empty. The blessing seems to touch a portion of our life for a moment, but we experience no sustained victory. The same struggles seem to reappear and we wonder why. The same thought patterns reemerge; the same emotional strains and cycles repeat and we feel defeated all over again. Why? Because we have allowed the worship from the altar of our heart to become contaminated through our weakened faith because of our life experiences. When was the last time you saw victory on your timeline? When was the last time you worshiped God from a place of sincerity? Do you still need victory in an area of your life, and if so, have you worshiped God in faith?

In faith, we bring our heart in alignment with who God is in our daily living, our present day. This is why the word of God says He is our present help in the time of need (Psalms 46:1). We are able to believe in what we cannot see, even under the most trying of situations and circumstances when we employ faith in worship. Abraham was able to believe God even though he had no visual evidence that what he believed for would manifest. His hope was in what God had promised him years before, but his faith had to rise to a new level. Why? Because up until that moment, his faith had been anchored in a past timeline event where God had spoken a word. But now that faith was being tested and proved in his present day, what would Abraham choose to hold onto: his hope in God or the circumstances of his current situation? Would Abraham faint in his heart and be overcome with despair, missing out on an opportunity to worship God? This was Abraham's chance to proclaim the power of God for generations to come, to seal the covenant between God and his people. Abraham did not faint in his heart; he did not allow his heart to become overwhelmed with despair; therefore, he prevailed in faith and as a result saw the present day blessing of God on that mountain. He worshiped God, and upon the altar, a nation was established through his seed.

CHAPTER SEVEN

Flash Backs

Think back for just a moment to a time in your life when you experienced a struggle or trial. Take your mind to the five W's of this event; who, what, where, when, and why of this moment on your life timeline. The first four "W's" are easier to recall; however, the "why" may not come so easily. The "why" of a trial may not become clear to us until we have actually moved passed the event. This is a key to understanding the power of one's testimony.

Allow me to explain this statement. Think of a time in which you have experienced a powerful move of God in your life, a time where God showed up on your behalf. Do the same as before and identify the five "W's" of this moment on your timeline. Notice that the "why" is the turning point and is the actual highlight or joyous part of the event. The "why" tells the cause of the result or outcome of the event; the "why" is the testimony!

For example, some years ago, I was involved in a car accident where my car was totaled. The other driver did not yield the right of way at the stop sign and drove right out in front of me. I tried to avoid hitting the car, but there was not enough time. The collision caused my air bags to deploy; I could smell smoke almost immediately after the impact. I remember trying to move, but the left side of my body was numb and I could not feel any sensation in my feet. I was able to reach my cell phone, which had been in the center console. I must have been in shock because I could not remember at the time how to dial a phone number; I just sat there looking at the phone. I could hear sirens faintly in the background. I closed my eyes and began to pray and ask God to be with the other driver and to protect him or her. I asked God to steady my mind and allow me to remain calm. I was able to call my husband and tell him what happened and where I was. I don't remember many of the moments that followed that phone call, but I do remember hearing my husband's voice saying, "I'm here April, I love you baby, I'm here." I was taken by ambulance to the emergency room. I was there for several hours undergoing testing and imaging. I was in a lot of pain, but I was still calm and I could feel the peace of God. I was not afraid even though at the time I still had very little sensation on my left side. I just continued to pray and ask God for continued peace over my mind. Okay, did you miss the testimony? Were you waiting for me to tell you some miraculous story of how God touched my body and I got up and walked and all the pain disappeared? The testimony here in this story is how God touched my mind and gave me peace in the midst of a very disoriented and chaotic time. He gave me peace, so that I could pray and seek Him, so that no matter what the outcome I could keep my mind and heart focused on Him. This is the result, the joyous part of this story; God gave me peace! I want you to know that I did receive healing in my body, and I was completely pain free within three days of the accident. Praise the Lord!

When we flash back to a past moment, we should be able to do so with a testimony. If your "why" does not bring glory to God, it is a place where you have not allowed God to exist, an unholy altar. Ok, let's explore the word "testimony" to obtain an even greater understanding. The word "testimony" means "to bear witness to, proof or evidence that something exist or is true" (Merriam-Webster Dictionary). Keeping this definition in mind, go back to the previous statement above: "If your 'why' does not bring glory to God, it is a place where you have not allowed God to exist." It's a place where you have not allowed your life to bear witness to God.

This is where the heart comes into play. When we recall a moment from our life timeline, the heart reacts. The heart's response will be based on its condition. The healthier the heart is, the greater the level of peace the heart is able to experience, which is evident in the form of the testimony. Ok, let's go back to the function of the heart revealed in Chapter three.

We discovered that the heart transports blood throughout the body, supplying every living cell with vital substances and nutrients; one of those life-sustaining substances is oxygen. The heart pumps the blood to the lungs where it is supplied with oxygen. The oxygenated blood then returns to the heart where it is then distributed back to the body. This cycle continues with each beat of the heart. The blood is combined with the oxygen, and together they supply every cell in the body with what is needed to sustain life. Likewise, the works of Christ are combined with the testimony, and together they supply every member in the "body" what is needed to sustain spiritual life. The response of the heart reveals the areas where we have overcome and also the areas where we still need the power to overcome.

When faced with discomfort and trials, we are presented with an opportunity for the true manifestation of God's existence in our life. The moment that we can identify the testimony, we have proof that God showed up! The moment we can share that testimony with others, we have proof that it's in the past! The only way for an event to be in the past on your timeline is for it to have not only a starting point, but also an outcome or identifiable end point. What does that mean for you? If you are still dealing with the pain, hurt, shame, anger, or secrets of a moment on your life timeline, it's not in your past; it's still very much in your present, and tomorrow it is in your future.

The Bible tells us that we overcome or conquer by means of the blood of the Lamb and by the word or utterance of our testimony (Revelation 12:11). This being true, we understand that our testimony is evidence of our faith and reliance in God and the hope that we have through the works of Christ. Our testimony empowers and builds up our faith because it is our internal proof that our hope in Christ is not misplaced and in fact is rewarded with life. As the Scriptures reveal,

> He who believes in the Son of God [who adheres to, trusts in, and relies on Him] has the testimony [possesses this divine attestation] within himself. He who does not believe God [in this way] has made Him out to be *and* represented Him as a liar, because he has not believed (put his faith in, adhered to, and relied on) the evidence (the testimony) that God has borne regarding His Son. And this is that testimony (that evidence): God gave us eternal life, and this life is in His Son. He who possesses the Son

has that life; he who does not possess the Son of God does not have that life (1 John 5:10–12, AMP).

If there is any testimony that we should be proud of, it is in knowing that our current situations are working in our favor, and that our faith in Christ enables us to have eternal life with God. So as you consider the events of your past, always remember that the testing and trying of your faith at those moments were only to produce a God-conscious testimony for you to share with others. Keeping this in mind will prevent your heart from entertaining fear and doubt, which can also affect your pure worship. And in the following chapter, we will observe how a doubtful heart can result in having an "unholy altar."

CHAPTER EIGHT

The Unholy Altar

A heart without faith cannot offer up true worship because its "altar" is contaminated with un-belief, fear, and doubt. The unholy altar is the result of a self-deceived heart. Man says within himself, "I am a good person, God knows what I have gone through, He knows how hard my life has been, and God knows all the pain I have endured." These all become the self-deceiving things we reiterate in order to excuse our bad behaviors, and deceitfully validate our lack of commitment to God. These self-deceptions prevent us from facing the truth about who we are. When we allow ourselves to remain in a deceived state of mind, we falsely believe that we are living an empowered life; hence, we never really experience God's true authority and power in our lives.

God's power enables us to overcome struggles, not tolerate them! The more we lie to ourselves about who we are, the longer it will take us to admit and face the things that cause us to live powerless lives. This is the result of an unholy altar; hence, we try to overcompensate for the lack of true power, and operate in the things mentioned earlier: manipulation, deceit, lies, twisting, misrepresentation, self-pity, false humility, fear, exaggerations, indulgent behaviors, and personal exhortations. All these things, when in full operation in the heart of an individual, produce an unholy altar on which man worships his own desires. Remember, the heart is designed to worship; therefore, it has all the integrated elements in which to worship without even having to think about it. This is why we have to guard our heart.

The Bible warns us that we must guard the heart because out of it flow the issues of life. Unholy altars cause us to doubt the word of God in our lives, and as a result, we disqualify ourselves from the blessing. We have to rid our lives of unholy altars in order to experience power-filled and victorious living, not just for a moment, but every day!

How do we get rid of the unholy altars in our lives? It starts with making a decision to make the word of God the final authority; we have to believe the word of God and then apply it. The word of God has to be our guiding post and measuring rod. We cannot allow life's experiences to hold a greater influence than the word of God; in fact, life experiences are called into subjection to the word of God. We have to move beyond the realm of sight and reaction in the flesh, and into the realm of faith and obedience in the spirit.

The realm of sight is living according to the human senses: what it looks like, tastes like, smells like, sounds like, and feels like. The realm of sight causes us to be reactive to outward stimuli that influence our physical responses. The realm of faith is living according to our knowledge of the Word of God. The realm of faith asks us to be obedient to what we know.

The unholy altar is a direct result of living in the realm of sight, relying on our own intellect, emotions, and feelings to navigate through life and to make decisions. We have to resist the pull to revert to our own human senses and reasoning, and keep our heart anchored in the word of God. This is not easy; it takes discipline and commitment to study and meditate on the word of God. The cornerstones of the unholy altar are fear, doubt, and unbelief; but the cornerstones of the holy altar are love and faith, which are gained through the word of God. The unholy altar has to be torn down, stone by stone, and replaced with the word of God that is received by faith. The Word of God says it this way:

> And I will give them singleness of heart and put a new spirit within them. I will take away their stony, stubborn heart and give them a tender, responsive heart, so they will obey my

decrees and regulations. Then they will truly be my people, and I will be their God (Ezekiel 11:19-20).

If we are to ever experience the victory that we have in Christ, we must be willing to accept this new heart that God provides, and allow His word to cleanse and purify our will, thoughts, and emotions.

CHAPTER NINE

The Mind and Heart Connection

The connection between the mind and the heart is very powerful. It's like breathing and oxygen. We can inhale, but if there is no oxygen in the atmosphere, our lungs are unable to take in what it needs to keep us alive. The lungs are not the problem; the lack of oxygenated air makes our lungs ineffective. This is the connection between what our mind perceives and the heart believes.

The mind can perceive or understand the word of God, but if the heart fails to receive or believe the word of God, then its knowledge is of no effect in our lives. The mind is a powerful step in restoring the altar of the heart; it's the gateway through which the word of God is received into the life of an individual. It's here in the mind that the first attempt of the enemy is made. He knows that if he can get you to reason with the word of God, then he can also prevent it from moving into the heart where true transformation takes place.

The human mind is powerful; it can be very difficult to override the desire to use human reasoning because it comes naturally to the flesh. This is because faith is not a function of the mind, but rather of the heart. The mind is the place where the enemy has to show up because he knows if he cannot stop the word of God here, he cannot stop it from working in our life. Once the word of God reaches the heart in faith, the seed of the word takes root, growing and flourishing through our faith, resulting in a victorious life. When the enemy comes against us in our minds, he is not after our human reasoning or personal intellect; he is not trying to prevent our own thoughts from emerging. Quite the contrary, this is exactly what he wants to promote. The enemy only comes against our minds to prevent the root of the knowledge of the word of God from entering in the heart. The fact of the matter is once the word reaches the heart, it changes the entire life of an individual, including the mind. The mind starts to perceive differently than before. The mind now becomes submissive to the leading of the heart because faith is now the default function instead of reasoning; and as a result, the function of the heart overrides the function of the mind. The heart, functioning in faith, now influences the way in which the mind perceives. The individual now has filters which they are able to pass all thoughts through and soberly discern what to hold onto and what to let go. These filters are faith and belief in the word of God; any thought that presents itself in direct conflict to faith is rejected and cast down.

> Well, I am begging you now so that when I come I won't have to be bold with those who think we act from human motives. We are human, but we don't wage war as humans do. We use God's mighty weapons, not worldly weapons, to knock down the strongholds of human reasoning and to destroy false arguments. We destroy every proud obstacle that keeps people from knowing God. We capture their rebellious thoughts and teach them to obey Christ (2 Corinthians 10:5).

This is why, as revealed earlier; the heart reveals the true person.

The heart provides a clear picture of who we are and what we truly believe. When life experiences occur on our timeline, and we have to make the choice to forgive wrongs and overcome oppositions, what is our heart conversation? Do we default to our senses to tell us how to respond, or do we rely on faith to direct us and keep our hearts and minds anchored in the word of God? The fact is we will experience trials, tests, and even painful situations in life; however, it's not the event that determines our heart's condition; it's what we allow God to do with them. We can allow God to take our life's journey and turn it into opportunities of true worship. It does not take very much effort to rejoice in times of plenty and celebration; it takes every effort to worship in times of trials.

The unholy altar is erected with very little effort in our lives; it is a result of a sick heart that has not yet been yielded to the power of faith and true belief in the word of God. The good news: The cure has already been given to us through Christ; we just have to make the decision to allow God to be Lord of our life. We have to surrender our entire heart to Him, especially the hidden secret places.

These are the places God desires most. When God reveals the unholy altar within our heart, it is a time of joy and celebration. The fact is we cannot address what we don't acknowledge. Having a true conversation within ourselves allows us to strip ourselves naked before the Lord, and to face who we really are. Acknowledging our issues is a positive first step in our process in overcoming and living a victorious life. The truth is we have to stop pretending to be an overcomer; we need to allow Christ to lift us over our stumbling blocks and experience true victory through Him. Stop allowing the enemy to gain a foothold over your mind and heart; it's time to address the hidden places where we have allowed ourselves to remain "lord;" it's time to surrender them. No more unholy sacrifices made on the unholy altars of the heart. Give it to the Lord and watch what a beautiful masterpiece he will give in return. I have determined that from now on, "My Heart will trust in the LORD."

CHAPTER TEN

Reflection

"As in water the face of man is reflected, so the heart reveals the true man" (Proverbs 4:23). The heart is the mirror of our life; it reflects back to us our true image. In order for us to know our heart's condition, we have to be honest within ourselves about who we are and our struggles. We cannot continue to allow self-deception to fog up the mirror and cloud the reflection. When the Lord reveals to us areas of our life that have not experienced true victory, it's not a time for regret or shame; it's a time of celebration. We have to remember that we cannot address what we have not acknowledged; before we can tear down the unholy altars, we first have to know they exist. Identifying unholy altars is a process in which we have an honest conversation with ourselves before God; it's a personal journey that we have to take. When I took this journey, the Lord revealed to me that my overly sensitive reaction to others' opinions of me did not bring Him glory, and in fact prevented me from experiencing a closer walk with Him. This was my starting point in identifying my unholy altars. This starting point would now take me on a seven year journey where I was able to explore my life timeline and uncover the cause of my over sensitivity. I had no idea when I started out on this journey that it would go so deep and that it would take so long; but the deeper I went, the more honest I had to be with myself. Every new discovery along my life timeline brought me closer to the truth of my heart's condition; my heart was sick and plagued with unholy altars. I asked myself ten questions (listed below) and each honest answer would lead me deeper into discovering my true self. There were some questions that I was able to answer quickly, but there were others I had to consider and think on for days at a time.

As you begin your journey, prepare to be completely honest with yourself and allow God to help you move through the process. Pray and allow your faith to increase through reading and meditating on the word of God each day. Remember this process is a personal journey that only you can take; listen to your heart as it begins to speak to you; it will reveal its true self if you are willing to hear.

Reflection Questions

Use these questions to help guide you through discovery and do not skip the questions. Answer each one honestly and completely; take as long as you need on each question.

1. What do I want people to know about me? Why is this important to me? (Read Colossians 4:5-6; Psalms 34:1-3.)

   _____
   _____
   _____
   _____
   _____

2. What do I believe people think about me? Why is this important to me? (Read Philippians 2:1-11 NLT.)

3. What don't I want people to know about me? Why is this important to me? How would I respond if people knew this? (Read Proverbs 28:13; Luke 8:17; Romans 8:1; 1Peter 5:6-11.)

4. What makes me unhappy about others? Why? Have I ever done this myself? (Read James 4:11-12; Matthew 6:14-15.)

5. What do I dislike most about myself? Why? Would I dislike this about others? Why or why not? (Read Ephesians 2:10; Psalms 139:13-18; 1 John 3:20.)

6. What do I find myself thinking about most of the time? Why is this so important to me? How does it

make me feel? (Read Romans 8:5-19; Philippians 4:6-8 NLT.)

7. What about me can I use to help others? How can I do this more often? Do I use this to help myself? (Read Romans 15:1-4; Galatians 6:3 NLT.)

8. What do I want to receive from others? Do I do this for others? (Read Proverbs 18:24; Proverbs 27:17.)

9. What is the hardest thing I ever had to forgive? Why was it so difficult? Have I forgiven this? (Read Romans 12:16-21; Ephesians 4:31-32 NLT.)

10. How do I know I love the Lord? How do I show that love to myself and others? (Read 1John 2:5; 1John 4:12-21 NLT.)

_____

_____

_____

_____

_____

Now that you have taken the first steps of your journey, do not stop here. Continue to seek the Lord for deeper understanding, and keep your heart open to receiving His instruction so that the Lord can reveal all the unholy altars in your life. Continue to ask the Lord to guide you through the process, and you will have victory where you did not have it before. Let the worship from your heart be a sweet aroma unto the Lord as you tear down every unholy altar.

> For we do not have a High Priest who is unable to understand and sympathize and have a shared feeling with our weaknesses and infirmities and liability to the assaults of temptation, but one who has been tempted in every respect

as we are, yet without sinning. Let us then fearlessly and confidently and boldly draw near to the throne of grace (the throne of God's unmerited favor to us sinners), that we may receive mercy [for our failures] and find grace to help in good time for every need [appropriate help and well-timed help, coming just when we need it] (Hebrews 4:15-16, AMP).

~Journal~